This book is dedicated to the members of St. Bartholomew's Episcopal Church, Nashville, and to the people of other parishes or denominations who participate in our weekly "Growing in the Spirit" prayer and praise group and our daily 6:15 A.M. Holy Communion and continental breakfast. These people are holding fast to the fundamentals of the Faith, and their example and their prayers have played a large role in the writing of this book.

George C. Thomas

FUNDAMENTALS
OF
THE
FAITH

Chuck Murphy

ABINGDON PRESS
Nashville, Tennessee

Fundamentals of the Faith

Copyright © 1976 by Abingdon Press

Library of Congress Cataloging in Publication Data

MURPHY, CHUCK, 1922-
  Fundamentals of the faith.

  1. Christian life—Anglican authors. 2. Theology, Doctrinal—Popular works. I. Title.
BV4501.2.M85   230′.1   75-30505

ISBN 0-687-13699-7

Manufactured by the Parthenon Press at
Nashville, Tennessee, United States of America

PREFACE

The Christian life is not based on a set of rules, nor is it a religion of ethics—although it does contain certain ethics. It is a way of life based on the Person of Jesus Christ, in response to His command to love, to be His witness, and to represent Him in His ministry and mission to the world. The first, and basic, requirement is a personal commitment to Him as Lord and Savior. He has provided great benefits for life on earth and has promised eternal life with God. Faith in Him is expressed in obedience to Him. Fulfillment of the commission He has given to His church requires the guidance and the power of the Holy Spirit, plus the "armor of God" which has been provided.

There are certain Christian absolutes that are unchanging, as well as certain "pat answers" to problems and situations that Christians are called upon to face. As the words to the old love song have it, the "fundamental things apply, as times goes by." It is when these absolutes are denied or ignored and when these pat answers are unbelieved that our happiness and fulfillment are diminished and the power to live the abundant life is dissipated.

This book was written to help people recall the fundamentals of the Christian faith so that they may enjoy the benefits that it gives and accept the responsibilities that it places upon those who profess Jesus Christ as Lord and Savior.

This book is as much a product of the mind, knowledge, and commitment of my wife, Anne, as it is of mine. She and the Holy Spirit are coauthors of it. I am deeply grateful to both of them for their help and encouragement.

CHUCK MURPHY

CONTENTS

FUNDAMENTALS OF THE FAITH

I have been called—accusingly by some of my fellow clergymen and approvingly by many members of the laity—a fundamentalist. Although I disapprove of pigeonholing a person through stereotyping or labeling, I consider this classification of me to be a compliment. If you spell fundamentalist with a small "f" and not a capital "F," I accept this term for myself. There is a difference between being a literalist and a fundamentalist, although many people incorrectly use the terms interchangeably. I am a fundamentalist when it comes to the fundamentals of the Christian faith. I believe in God as a loving Creator-Father. I believe that Jesus Christ is the way—the only way—to salvation. I believe that the Bible was inspired by God, that it contains the Word of God, and that it speaks to any and every situation today. I believe that prayer is heard and answered by God. I also believe that it is the most powerful force man has at his disposal. I know that when a person commits his life to Jesus Christ and allows Him to rule his life—affecting every decision he makes—this person becomes a new person. He receives the Holy Spirit and His gifts. He begins to experience the abundant life that Jesus brings and to exercise the

9

power that came at Pentecost. If I did not and could not believe these things, I would renounce my ministry.

Whether or not these fundamentals speak to and affect a person's life depends on whether or not that person knows God, has accepted Jesus Christ as his personal Lord and Savior, and has claimed the gifts and the power of the Holy Spirit. That person must also read God's holy word, pray to the God it reveals, and be prepared to participate in the ministry and witness of those who profess to belong to Jesus Christ.

It is particularly disturbing to me that there are things being taught in some seminaries and espoused by some clergymen that are denials of the fundamentals of the Christian faith. Recently a "minister" stated publicly that the Bible never says that Jesus is God and that it would be inaccurate both historically and theologically to portray the Christian position as asserting that Jesus is God. This was reported by the Richmond (Virginia) *Times-Dispatch* in November, 1974.

In response to a flurry of letters to the paper which were critical of this statement, another clergyman, in defense of it, said that those critical letters represent a particular view of Christianity known variously as literalist or fundamentalist or conservative. He stated that the writers might be surprised to learn that many Christians, clergy and lay, from many denominations recite the traditional creeds regularly and hold them firmly as summaries of Christian truth but do not believe them to be factual statements. He said, "Mr. _____ and his teachings fit well within the Anglican

Communion which has combined over the centuries the old, the new, and the open; church, Bible, and common sense; tradition, scripture, and reason; Catholic, Protestant, and human. Many of Mr. _____'s teachings are privately held by many clergy. He is to be commended for making his views known. . . . Mr. _____ is an effective missionary to intellectual moderns who have been alienated by fundamentalistic views held by many Christians.''

I deny vehemently that his teaching fits well within the Anglican Communion. I do not deny that there are some clergymen who do not believe some of the basic tenets of the Christian faith. I assert that Mr. _____'s statement is a denial of the basic fact upon which Christianity stands. If Jesus was just a man, then his death had no effect, and we are thrown back on the impossible requirement that we must save ourselves. If Jesus was not God incarnate, then all the other Christian truths have no validity, and Christianity is a cruel hoax.

It seems to me that any clergyman who recites the Christian creeds without meaning what he is saying automatically makes himself a liar. Not only is he a fraud, but he has also reneged on the solemn vow that he made at his ordination. The honorable thing to do would be to renounce the ministry and call himself a deist, unitarian, or humanist. Although he needs our prayers, my real concern is the effect that he and the others who agree with him are having on the congregations they serve.

I have the same deep concern about the effect that

some of the teaching at some of the seminaries is having on some of the students. The alarming fact is that the students who believe everything that is being taught are eventually going to be turned loose on congregations. If they teach, preach, and promote what they have been taught, the Christian faith will have been watered down, and its life-changing effect will be seriously hampered.

One of my sons graduated in May, 1975, after three rough years in seminary. Those years were made rough because he believes that the Christian faith does have the answers, that the Bible is the Word of God, that Christianity is not just one among many equally good religions, that private prayer brings results, and that prayer groups can be powerfully effective. Because he would not back down on his beliefs, he was considered unteachable by some of the faculty, who gave the impression of not only being ultraliberal, but man-centered instead of Christ-centered. I like to believe that every man who enters seminary goes there believing the basic tenets of Christianity, but what about those who are teachable and are persuaded to "sell out"? I have known men to leave the seminary because they had lost their faith completely. This is unfortunate, but not nearly as tragic as the ones who lose their faith but continue in the seminary, graduate, are ordained, and then become the "spiritual" leaders of congregations.

As a matter of principle, I resent the hypocrisy of those clergy who privately deny the faith which they publicly profess. I also resent the arrogant opportunists who publicly deny their faith but continue to enjoy the privileges of their position in the church. I believe it is dishonest for a minister to stay in the ordained ministry while not believing what must be openly professed when reciting the creeds. It is just as dishonest for a layperson to behave in this manner.

"God is still not mocked." That biblical truth holds, and proof of it can be found in the fact that the churches whose members believe in the creeds are growing, and the others are not. It is also true that ministers who believe in the creeds find that they have an effective ministry, and others who do not, do not.

Nostalgia has been popular the last few years. Fashions from the Roaring Twenties, the thirties, and the forties have taken over the clothing world. Movies about these eras, such as *The Sting*, *Bonnie and Clyde*, *Paper Moon*, and *The Great Gatsby*, have attracted long lines to the box offices. Broadway has seen revivals of *No, No, Nanette and Irene;* and *Over Here*, with the Andrews Sisters reliving the days of USO canteens during World War II, has been a smash hit. My youngest son was telling me today that a young man who runs a record shop was impressed that many young people were discreetly, and almost furtively, buying albums of the music of the big band era. I realize that human memory tends to forget the bad and remember only the good of bygone days. But I believe this looking-backward trend is a subconscious desire for a life that is believed to have been more simple—a life with certain clearly defined absolutes which seem to us now to represent a sense of security. After all, our world is often hectic, bewildering, and mixed-up.

In the same way, people are looking for and rediscovering the basic fundamentals of the Christian faith. After years of floundering, and, in a real sense deifying man, many people are discovering that man is not and cannot be God. They have found that man alone cannot control his destiny nor manage his life successfully. People are discovering that individually or corporately they cannot cope with life's problems without help from something outside themselves—something more powerful and wiser.

It has been reported that while overall church membership and attendance is down, membership, attendance, and commitment are increasing in churches where the Bible is preached, where the fundamentals of Christianity are taught, and where people are challenged to total commitment to Jesus Christ. A child with no guidance, no restrictions, and with no demands on him grows up insecure and bewildered. Even when he fights against advice, restrictions, and demands, those things are settling into his subconscious. As he grows older he realizes that they are forms of love and concern. God who is love, advises, restricts, and demands because He has nothing but love for His children. The worst thing parents can say to a child is "I don't care what you do." That means they do not love him. The worst thing that God could say to us is "I don't care what you do." Christian love (God's kind of love) says, "I *will* the best for you, and I'm willing to be used to get it for you." That was the kind of love Jesus had for us, and the Cross was proof of it. God wills only the best for us. He is our loving Heavenly Father. There are times when His love is "tough" love, because He is willing to go to any lengths to get us to enjoy life with Him—the abundant life. People who believe the fundamentals of the Christian faith grow deeper in it because they realize that this is God's plan for us.

Last year ended with the news media reporting a serious recession as inevitable, inflation growing daily, and unemployment climbing. In the parish where I am the minister, our attendance at worship services and Sunday school has never been higher, our canvass showed the 1975 pledges to be over 20 percent higher than those for 1974. Our outreach to those outside our parish and the ministry of our members is becoming much like what I imagine the early church to have been. I am convinced that this has happened because Jesus Christ is allowed to be the Lord of this parish, the Bible is preached and taught, the Holy Spirit is allowed to rule and direct many of our lives, and Christ's commands are being obeyed. The people are taking seriously the vows that they made to God when they were baptized and/or confirmed.

When you see people believing and living by the fundamentals of Christian faith, you can see in them the fruits and the power of the Holy Spirit. When you see those people who have committed their lives to Jesus enjoying the abundant life, having their prayers answered, and exhibiting the power that Jesus promised, it becomes undeniably clear that those people are on to something.

It is a thrilling thing to see people come to know Jesus as a living person, and through Him come to know God. In knowing Jesus, they come to know what God is like. People sometimes say that the God of the Old Testament and the God of the New Testament are different. God remains always the same. It is man's understanding of God that changes. Until Jesus, God seemed remote and unknowable, but Jesus is the revelation of God. Any other way of trying to know what God is like is speculation. He came to show us that God is love; that He offers forgiveness, acceptance, understanding and concern. These are the attributes that Jesus of Nazareth manifested in His earthly life. He was so much more than just an example. He was *the* example in living a life of love, forgiveness, acceptance, understanding, and concern. People who have committed their lives to Jesus Christ inevitably exhibit His traits in their lives and in their relationships with other people.

The purpose of this book is to help the nominal Christian come to know God through Jesus Christ. Its goal is to encourage people to use the Bible as God's personal instruction manual for daily life, to allow the Holy Spirit to change and rule their personal lives, and to enjoy the power and the comfort of prayer. This will lead them to witness to and evangelize others, so that the gospel will be proclaimed, the kingdom spread, and Jesus Christ will be acknowledged as Lord and Savior of the world.

Faith is never something that is original with us. It is both a gift and a fruit of the Holy Spirit. Faith as a gift is received when we are baptized and/or accept Jesus Christ as our personal Lord and Savior. Faith as a fruit of the Holy Spirit becomes evident as we allow Jesus to be the Lord of our lifes and permit the Holy Spirit to guide and direct our lives. But what causes us to be baptized or to accept Jesus as our Lord and Savior? The apostolic faith, as stated in the Christian creeds, is the faith that has been handed down to us from the apostles. St. Paul, in the seventeenth verse of the tenth chapter of his letter to the Romans, says: "So faith comes from what is heard, and what is heard comes by the preaching of Christ." From the beginning of Christianity, the fundamentals of the Christian faith have been handed down through the Bible and through the preaching and witnessing of people who believed those fundamentals and experienced what they promised. The church has gone astray every time it has gotten away from these fundamentals.

In your own community, can you see lives changed? Are the gifts and the fruits of the Spirit being manifested in the church members? And most of all, is love among the members obvious to everyone? Is outreach to those outside the fellowship one of your church's main objectives? If these things are not evident in your church, I am positive that the fundamentals of Christianity are being neglected there. I am also convinced that when the fundamentals are neglected, or are not given the priority they deserve, bickering, fault-finding, hurt feelings, and cliques serve to destroy the "family" atmosphere in the church, and the work of the church is hindered or ceases.

In the next few chapters, the fundamentals will be discussed, and the final chapter will deal with witnessing—primarily the witness that is taking place among the laity in such things as the charismatic movement, Faith Alive, Faith at Work, renewal weekends, and "prayer and share" groups. In any and all instances, the work of the church is never done by people who have not put on the armor of God. The armor of God is for the protection of the Christian, and its purpose is to aid him in the battle for the souls of people.

JESUS CHRIST—
THE ALL-IMPORTANT
FUNDAMENTAL

Jesus! Who is He? Why has He had such a profound effect upon history? Why does His name alone evoke such strong and varied emotions in people? In the first chapter of this book some sort of answer to these questions can be found. The stock answer immediately pops out—Jesus is the Son of God. Jesus is one of the three elements of the Trinity. Jesus is the Lord. Jesus is the Savior. Most people have heard these answers, even if some of them do not believe them. Both Christians and non-Christians acknowledge that a man named Jesus really did live in a small country called Palestine almost two-thousand years ago. It is an undeniable fact that His life has profoundly affected human history. Our calendar is based on His time on earth—divided into "before" and "after" he lived here. Morality and laws have been influenced by His teachings. Art, architecture, music, and literature have all reflected His influence. Millions of people have called themselves "Christian" in order to be identified as His followers. Few intelligent people would argue the fact that Jesus has made a tremendous impact on history and on the lives of millions of people. In view of this, I will attempt primarily to discuss some of the "why" questions rather than present the more basic Christian teachings about Him.

Why did He come to earth? Why was He born? According to Ephesians 1:9-12, God created man for a purpose. This purpose was apparently to love and praise God, and to live abundant and creative lives on earth as a prelude to eternal life in heaven. Both the Old and New Testaments contain numerous passages attesting to this purpose. Obviously, however, something has gone amiss. A study of secular or religious history will show that the majority of mankind has not achieved either of these goals. According to a recent newspaper article, out of the past 3,462 years there has been only 230 years without war. A look at the contemporary scene is overwhelming evidence of man's failure. You can't miss it. Listen to the radio, watch TV, read the newspaper, or just look around your own little world. Man, on his own, does not progress according to God's plan for him. True, he does fairly well with some of the original instructions in Genesis 1:28, "fill the earth and subdue it; and have dominion over the fish of the sea and over the birds of the air and over every living thing that moves upon the earth." In recent time man has also taken dominion over the atom, many diseases, space travel, and areas undreamed of even a few decades ago. Man's difficulty does not stem from a lack of achievement. It goes much deeper. Genesis 2:7 says, "Then the Lord God formed man of dust from the ground, and breathed into his nostrils the breath of life; and man became a living being." This sentence is a magnificent summary of

God's dream for man. God didn't create man simply to be of the earth—of the flesh, with the meeting of human needs as the final goal. No! From the very beginning God envisioned so much more for man. He breathed His own Spirit into us. We were created by and for the Spirit of God. The ultimate purpose was for us to become God's people—not just His creatures, but a higher creation capable of a relationship with our Creator. Man discovered, in the beginning, as well as today, that of all the things God has given him, the gift of free will is the most tempting, the most intoxicating and exhilarating. So naturally he tries it out first. It's so good to be free! To be free to be me! But this tempting thing is also a dangerous thing because the misuse of it can be so devastating. From Adam and Eve to you and me, mankind really has not changed much.

All this is a preliminary to answer the question "Why did Jesus come to earth?" The answer is obvious. Because man had lost sight of God's purpose for him, and the gulf that had developed between him and God had become too deep for him to bridge. His use of his freedom had become misuse of his freedom. He had rebelled against any form of order or discipline that thwarted his own desires. His "free to be me" attitude always seemed to end in chaos, in deterioration of his relationships with other people, and eventually in a sense of futility in his life. What had started out to be a joyful, free-swinging existence had become a nightmare of frustration. Man was in a maze of his own making with no sense of direction and with all the corridors leading to dead ends.

In the Bible's telling of man's adventures there is always a faithful remnant who cling to the vision of God's purpose for them. In our individual lives I think there is always a faithful remnant of God's Spirit in us that makes us cling to a hope of something more—a higher purpose for our lives. This becomes a persistent conviction of our need for help. In the choas and the "lostness" of estrangement and frustration we begin to perceive that we need a savior. It is to this need of mankind's that Jesus came and still comes. In the Bible, only those who admitted their need for a savior accepted Jesus. It is no different today. God doesn't force us into a relationship with Him, but He has provided the way back through Jesus Christ.

"If God sent Jesus to show me how to find purpose for my life—how to make sense out of this nonsense—then why isn't my life different now?" This question is more common in the minds of Christians than we may realize because most people never actually ask this out loud. A basic misconception in the churches today seems to be that all those enjoying good fortune are really Christian. This misconception may provide some difficulties for the church—especially with such things as attendance, support of the church, and unity and harmony in the church body—but, the most tragic consequences are to the individual members. Many of those who assume that they are Christians have never had any real encounter with the Lord and have never consciously and verbally accepted Jesus as their personal Lord and Savior. Some of these people go through the motions of church membership for years

22

and secretly wonder why this doesn't make more difference in their lives. Others get discouraged or disillusioned with church and just drop out. Still others, and they are more fortunate, find themselves in an impossible situation in their lives and out of sheer desperation begain to ask questions and seek help.

Even at this point, sometimes there are pitfalls. In seeking to help, a well-meaning Christian who wants to tell a friend that help really is available and that the Lord is both able and eager to work in a person's life can be trapped with words. I don't know what the answer is, because the words "Accept Jesus Christ as your Savior, turn your life over to Him, and allow Him to be your Lord" are absolutely true. I don't know any other way to say this. Yet, I realize that these words can sound very threatening to some people. Where they should bring hope, they can bring hostility or despair. To some people they seem to sound either impossible or impractical as agents of help in their particular situation. There are various reasons for this type of reaction. None of them is valid enough to excuse a Christian from making some sort of witness about the Lord to a person who asks for help. All of us get caught in the "I'll have to do something about this situation" trap. It is humbling to have to say, "I really don't know what to tell you to do, but I know that God has helped me out of a lot of difficult spots, and I know that He will help you, if you will let Him." This is a form of stepping aside to allow God to work. It is giving Him the praise, instead of building our own egos by giving lots of good advice. The surest way to keep from coming into a relationship with Jesus Christ, or to keep others from it, is to keep trying to understand the Christian fundamentals with our intellect.

We can ponder, argue, meditate, reflect, and debate upon Christian teachings, and we still reach either no conclusion or many differing ones. The hard fact of the matter is that we can know no part of Almighty God except as He reveals Himself to us. This is a hard, frustrating thing for arrogant men to grasp and accept. Jesus knew this. He accepted the limitations of humanity. He went ahead and forged the way for us. He *is* the Way. His words "No man comes to the Father except by me" are the key for us. We must accept our human limitations just as Jesus accepted His. Once we accept this, Christian teaching makes sense. John 8:32 tells us, "You will know the truth, and the truth will make you free." The truth really does make us free. Free to accept what God has provided for us, free to relax and stop trying to do everything in our own strength, free to use any method that is most helpful to us in making a commitment of our lives to Him.

One woman I know wrote down on a piece of paper, with the date and place, her initial confession of faith. She tells me this has helped her when she begins to doubt. She can reread what she has written, and accept it as fact. She is no longer subject to her feelings or fears in the matter. Several people have told that their first real relationship with Jesus came as the result of their angry outbursts to God, when they had reached such points of desperation in their lives that they simply said out loud, "God, if you are real, show me! I'm mad, and I hurt. I don't believe you are a God who cares. If you are, do something!" This may have been the first time these people had ever really been honest either with God or about God. God always honors honesty. Many people have come into real relationships with God through other people who have been willing to be vulnerable with them by sharing their lives at a level that could be identified with. Jesus is the Way, but He waits for each of us to come to Him in the way that enables us best to accept Him.

This is why it is so important for Christians to be willing to share with other people what Jesus has done for them or what He means to them. It is not a matter of "collecting scalps" for the Lord. It is simply a matter of obeying His command to "be my witnesses." It isn't our problem whether or not our witness is effective. The important thing is that we are obedient and that we act in love. God doesn't ask us to be successful, He asks us to be obedient. He asks us to do His work in love—His kind of love, and remember God's kind of love is to will the best for the other person and to be willing to be used by God to achieve this best for him.

Regardless of how long a person has had a relationship with Jesus or how much he has studied the Bible, attended Church, or study courses, there is always more to learn. The entire Christian life is one of learning. In Matthew 11:29, Jesus says: "Take my yoke upon you, and learn from me; for I am gentle and lowly in heart, and you will find rest for your souls." As we ask and allow Him to, He will teach us more and more of the things that will enable us to live life to the fullest.

25

By yoking ourselves with the Son of God, we find ourselves being taken from one glorious adventure to another as He begins to turn even the commonplace or mundane events of our lives into "life more abundant." He has always been able to do extraordinary things with ordinary people who put their trust in Him and offer Him their obedience.

What has He been doing in your life recently? What have you allowed Him to do in your life recently?

His original reason for coming was to do something wonderful in the lives of people who would allow Him to. He wants to make something beautiful of our lives.

THE HOLY SPIRIT

In this book I have deliberately not written a chapter on God. This is better left to the theologians. To me, God the Creator-Father is the "given" factor, while the fundamentals are for the purpose of helping us come to God, worship God, and serve God. In the previous chapter the subject was Jesus Christ, the Savior, Redeemer, Mediator, God-Revealer, and most important, the way to God. This chapter is on the third element of the Trinity: the Holy Spirit; Strengthener, Guide, Empowerer, "God-in-Action."

One mistake that many Christians make—either out of carelessness or ignorance—is to call the Holy Spirit "It." The Holy Spirit is a Person. In the Old Testament accounts, the Holy Spirit fell on certain individuals in order to equip them to fulfil certain tasks God had called them to do. He is the Presence of God who empowers, guides, and directs God's people when they allow Him to do so. After His ascension, Jesus sent the Spirit to His followers to guide and strengthen them in carrying on His ministry and mission to the world. He resides in the church; the Body of Christ, the fellowship of believers. We commit our lives to Jesus the Christ; our goal is the right relationship with God the Father, but it is God the Holy Spirit whose presence we experience and who deals directly with us.

There have been times in the past when the Holy Spirit has been the neglected—if not forgotten—element of the Trinity. This might explain why the Christian church has not moved "like a mighty army" the way it was originally intended to do. I once had a lady tell me that she never understood all this business about the Holy Spirit, so she just put the whole thing out of her mind. I am afraid that that was more the rule than the exception in the past, but for the past fifteen years or so, the Holy Spirit has "come into His own"—and that's not just a pun. His importance and function is being better understood, acknowledged, and called upon, and His gifts are being more widely claimed.

His purpose is to glorify Christ, to enable us to know Jesus, to lead believers into all truth, and to reveal meaning in the Scriptures. He came to give the power to live and share the abundant life through new birth, to interpret our prayers, to make our witness effective, to strengthen us, and to be our advocate before God. If the majority of Christians in the past have ignored, denied, or not understood who the Holy Spirit is and what His function is, it is little wonder that Christianity has not done what Jesus Christ commissioned His church to do. Unless a gift of any kind is accepted and used for its intended purpose, nothing much happens. Many people in the past have treated the Holy Spirit the way some people treat valuable jewels. They have them vaulted away, but never wear them. People receive the Holy Spirit when they are baptized and/or when they accept Jesus as their Lord and Savior. Many people sort of store Him away as something that comes with the package of being a Christian, and they do not allow Him to do His work in or with them.

A gift from God is not a reward but a sign of a relationship. God adopts us when we commit our lives to Jesus; He gives us a task and equips us for it. The gift of the Holy Spirit, and the power He brings, is the way God works in, on, and through His people. In I Corinthians 12:8-10, St. Paul lists the gifts of the Spirit. Unfortunately they are not always claimed and used—but even more unfortunate is the fact that they are sometimes misused and abused. The only way that we can tell that we are using them correctly is when the fruits of the Spirit are evident in us. There is also a hunger for and appreciation of God's word as well as a desire for fellowship with other Christians.

The fruits of the Spirit are the character and nature of Christ being manifested in His people. Galatians 5:22-23 lists the fruits of the spirit: love, joy, peace, patience, gentleness, kindness, faith, humility, and discipline. The entire thirteenth chapter of I Corinthians is about the central fruit of the Spirit: love. *Christian love* (agape) *is proof of authenticity.* If love is not evident in a person who manifests one or more of the gifts, the gifts may well become demonic. The fruits of the Spirit need to be seen in order to show people what Jesus is like and to show that He loves them. The world must see Jesus in those who belong to Him. What has been called the "baptism of the Spirit" is simply the outflowing of this love. The only way we can show our love for God is by loving our fellowman. As we mature in His love, we can reach out to love not only other Christians but the unbeliever and the enemy.

The gifts of the Holy Spirit may be divided into three classes:

I. The Power to Know (the gifts of revelation)
  A. the gift of knowledge
  B. the gift of wisdom
  C. the discerning of spirits

II. The Power to Do (gifts of power)
  A. the gift of faith
  B. the working of miracles
  C. the gift of healing

III. The Power to Say (inspirational gifts)
  A. the gift of prophecy
  B. the gift of tongues
  C. the interpretation of tongues

The gift of knowledge is the supernatural revelation of facts not learned through the efforts of the natural mind. It is the mind of Christ manifested to a believer *when needed* for protection, for more effective praying, or for revealing an undisclosed need that someone has. This knowledge comes through the Holy Spirit to our spirits, and it is always given for a purpose. It is important to know, and it can be helpful to us. We must keep in mind that Jesus Christ laid aside his omniscience in His incarnation and thus met situations through the Holy Spirit as we are to do. This gift is not human ability, it is not developed, but comes straight from God.

A lady in our church was late one day for a mid-week prayer group. She was traveling much too fast down a narrow street when suddenly something told her to slow down. She immediately slowed down almost to a halt, and had she not done so it could have been fatal, for around a sharp curve was a truck stalled in the middle of the road. There is no use trying to walk with the Lord unless we are willing to listen to Him and obey Him. Another friend of mine was late in leaving Birmingham for Nashville, so he really put a heavy foot on the gas pedal in hopes of making up some time. As he started up a long hill outside Cullman, Alabama, an ambulance passed him with its red lights flashing. He didn't give it too much thought, but continued about sixty-five miles an hour up the hill. All of a sudden an audible voice, as if there were someone in the car with him, said "slow down" and called him by name. He immediately took his foot off the gas and coasted to the top. Even with this he had to slam on the brakes, for just over the rise of the hill were two wrecked cars and the ambulance completely blocking the road.

Both of these incidents illustrate the gift of super-natural knowledge given for protection. I am sure that there are many people who can recall similar warnings of danger which they considered as premonitions, but did not recognize as coming from God. We sometimes forget or fail to realize that God wants the best for all His children, so we shouldn't be surprised at His gifts. Then too, there are many incidents when good Christians are not given this word of warning. Receiving the Holy Spirit is not an insurance policy against physical harm. I can't explain why some receive a warning and some do not, just as I cannot explain why some people are healed through prayer and the laying on of hands and some are not. I am sure there is a reason, but I think we should concentrate on, and be thankful for, the times the warnings or the healings do occur.

There are times when a person may receive a gift of supernatural knowledge that is puzzling. It may not be an order, as in the above cases, but simply "knowing" something. In this case, the gift of wisdom is needed in order to know what to do with whatever kind of knowledge God has given, for proper judgment for action. These two gifts go together and are usually given together. The gift of wisdom is manifested in sudden inspiration; interpretation of certain dreams, visions, and vocal gifts of the Holy Spirit; and sometimes in the audible voice of God. This supernatural word of wisdom is given to meet a particular situation, answer a particular question, or to utilize a particular piece of any kind of knowledge—natural or supernatural.

Jesus promised this to His followers, in Matthew 10:16-20: "Behold, I send you out as sheep in the midst of wolves; so be wise as serpents and innocent as doves. Beware of men; for they will deliver you up to councils, and flog you in their synagogues, and you will be dragged before governors and kings for my sake, to bear testimony before them and the Gentiles. When they deliver you up, do not be anxious how you are to speak or what you are to say; for what you are to say will be given to you in that hour; for it is not you who speak, but the Spirit of your Father speaking through you."

This is not an invitation to us to sit back and do nothing. We are supposed to acquire as much knowledge as we can. We are responsible for our intellectual knowledge and wisdom. God is responsible for our supernatural knowledge and wisdom.

I have been told about a man who went to seminary—and whether or not it is a true story doesn't matter, for it is a good illustration. One night before the first big exam, a group of the students were going to get together to study for it. They asked another man if he would like to join them, but he said, "No! I have prayed about it, and the Holy Spirit will speak to me and tell me what to say." The next morning, right after the test was over, his fellow seminarians asked him if the Holy Spirit spoke to him. He replied, "Yes! He told me that I hadn't done my homework."

This man made the mistake of standing on a promise that Jesus had not made, but there are times when the Holy Spirit does give us supernatural wisdom. It does not always come from the audible voice of God or from deep within ourselves, but from other people that God uses as His channels.

This can throw us off, particularly if He uses a small child. It can also challenge our faith or commitment when He uses a small child to put us to the test. One example of this is the true story of a family who were headed for the lake with their boat. When they arrived they discovered the acid had spilled out of the boat's battery. The disgruntled father said, "Now we'll have to drive all the way back into town and try to find some battery acid. This is going to really ruin our day for us." On the way back to town, their eight-year-old son said, "I wonder what would happen if we put some plain water in the battery and prayed that God would turn it into acid?" Of course this seemed pretty ridiculous to his parents, so his mother said, "If we had enough faith it might work." After riding along in somewhat strained silence, the child finally said, "Well, I've got faith." So, being put on the spot (for this family was very active in church work, prayer groups, spiritual renewal weekends), they turned around to hunt for some water. They put some water in the battery and prayed over it, and to the surprise of the parents, the motor started. This boy had the kind of child-like faith that all Christians are supposed to have. I believe that God honors faith just as He honored this young boy's faith. To me, it is irrelevant whether or not there is a logical explanation why this happened. God is the author of all logic, so it certainly should not be surprising if we discover logical explanations for His miracles. The point of this story is that we must step out on faith believing that God *will* act. Unless we are willing to trust Him enough to do this, we may never be aware of His activity in our lives. Unless we are willing to respond, we cannot appropriate any of God's gifts of the Holy Spirit. This is also the way we sometimes receive God's wisdom. All the gifts of the Spriit are powerful, but we must have the gift of wisdom in order to know what to do with them.

The gift of discernment is not the same as natural

discernment. Natural discernment is judgment we pass on people, situations, and circumstances; and it is derived from teachings we have received from home, environment, and culture. Like conscience, it is cultivated and shaped by various things, and it is not always reliable. Spiritual discernment comes from the mind being renewed by Jesus Christ. This grows through Christian fellowship, prayer, and the study of God's word. The Holy Spirit works in our minds—discarding the wrong and adding the right. This way our mind becomes more and more in agreement with the holy Scriptures, and the Holy Spirit within us.

The discerning of spirits is a "police" gift. Many Christians are not aware enough of the activities of Satan to be concerned about this—but they should be. This gift is the ability to know what is motivating a person or group. The believer recognizes the presence of the Holy Spirit in people and in situations. He can recognize the presence of evil as well. The presence of the Holy Spirit brings joy, love, and peace. The presence of a wrong spirit brings a sense of heaviness, unrest, tension, and anxiety. The principal purpose of this gift is to keep the enemy's influence from causing problems in the Christian fellowship.

This gift is particularly necessary when any of the other gifts of the Spirit are being manifested and when bringing deliverance to those who are bound by Satan. If you have ever attended a prayer and praise group, I am sure that there are times when things just don't feel right. You may not know what it is, but there is something unsatisfying about the meeting. Instead of being refreshed and joyful, you leave with a heaviness and a feeling of depression. A person who has been given the spirit of discernment will pick this up almost immediately. There needs to be prayer for knowledge and wisdom for guidance in handling this. It seems incongruous that this can happen among a group of Christians who are meeting for the express purpose of prayer and praise—but what better place for the devil to get his licks in? The devil is the great deceiver, and if he can plant dissension within a group of Christians, he has made great headway. The gift of discernment is like having certain trained dogs to discover smuggled heroin; it is a gift to "sniff out" any deceiving spirits that the devil may unleash.

The definition of the gift of faith is given in Hebrews 11:1: "the substance of things hoped for, the evidence of things not seen" (KJV). While natural human faith comes through the experience of the five senses, supernatural faith is above the natural senses and comes from God. Faith, as a gift, is given at the moment we receive Jesus as Lord and Savior. When that seed of faith is cultivated, fed, and watered through prayer, Bible reading, worship, and Christian fellowship, it becomes a fruit of the Spirit. The gift of faith has potential from the moment of accepting Jesus, but, like the other gifts, it becomes more active when the person is open to the Holy Spirit. The gift of faith is distinct from the working of miracles, but it may produce miracles. This gift of the Spirit is the ability to put people and situations in God's hands, while standing by ready to be used by God as His channel.

Miracles are events that seem to override or contradict so-called laws of nature. There are times that God will change His customary ways of doing things in order to meet His believers' needs and in order to show that he is sovereign, has all power, and is in control. The gift of miracles always brings glory to God. With the coming of the full power of the Holy Spirit, people should be seeing—and many people are seeing—miracles happening every day. Miracles always strengthen the faith of believers and encourage those who want to believe. There are documented proofs of modernday miracles in some of the less developed countries. I am convinced that these are occurring among new Christians because no one has told them to doubt that they would occur. It is tragic that in the more enlightened countries, Christians let intellect and sophistication block the Holy Spirit from having full sway. As we grow spiritually and as our commitment deepens, it will produce more and more miracles in our lives. Miracles are for the purpose of meeting the needs of God's children, and of leading others to Jesus Christ. Perhaps not as spectacular as some, but just as authentic, are the changed lives that we can see around us in the Christian fellowships. Many people do not see many miracles because they do not expect to see them, but if we expect to see them and look for them, we are apt to find that they are more common than we ever thought they could be.

The gift of healing is the most widely accepted of all the gifts, although there is still some resistance to or denial of this gift. More and more of the "mainline"

Christian denominations are beginning to take seriously the third part of Jesus' command for us to "preach, teach, and heal." Healings, like miracles, are the continuation of Jesus' ministry to people in need. The "laying on of hands" with prayer for healing serves as a point of contact for the sick to release their faith, and it is also a channel for spiritual power.

I believe that all prayers of petition should end with the words "if it be thy will," *except* in the area of sickness. There is no scriptural warrant to end our prayer with the faith-destroying "if it be thy will." Sickness is evil—not sinful. Although sin can make us sick, all sickness is not the result of sin. Sickness is evil, and to assume that God may want a person to be sick goes against His basic nature, which is love. God has made it clear in His word that it is His will to heal the sick. To pray for healing in a conditional manner is, in my opinion, an insult to God.

If you were to ask me to come to the hospital to see you and to pray for you, I would never put a condition on my prayer. I would say, "In the name of Jesus, be healed." I believe this is the only proper way to practice the gift of healing. Jesus and His disciples never assumed that God wanted a person sick. They never said, "Be healed, if it be God's will." They never refused to heal by saying something like, "Your suffering will help you develop character, and grow in faith." They knew that anything that harms or threatens God's people is evil. Evil is the enemy, God's and ours. This is not to say that some good cannot come from sickness that is not healed. I do not know why everyone who prays for healing is not healed, but I do know that God can redeem suffering and pain for His purpose, as He did with the Cross. He allows sickness, but He does not send sickness. God wants His people whole, in spirit, soul, and body. God is never glorified in the sickness of His people. One of the reasons I feel so strongly about this is the way God has healed in our church's midweek healing service and in our "Growing in the Spirit" prayer and praise group.

The gift of prophecy is supernatural speech in a known language. This gift is manifested when believers speak the mind of God by the inspiration of the Holy Spirit, not from their own thoughts. Prophecy is not a private gift. It is brought to and for a group of believers who must evaluate it. In I Corinthians 14:1-5, 39-40, St. Paul calls this the greatest of the gifts for the benefit of the Christian body. It has two purposes: the edification of believers and the reaching of unbelievers. It ministers to believers in three ways: edification, exhortation, and comfort.

Prophecy requires a great deal of faith on the part of the one prophesying because it requires him to speak out directly. All of us are reluctant to "make a fool of ourselves." Human pride and doubt, cause us to be reticent about speaking out. We should remember that the Scriptures say that any yielded child of God may be moved by the Holy Spirit to prophesy. Our prophecy is to be evaluated or judged by believers in terms of the witness of the Spirit in their hearts and in terms of whether the prophecy is in agreement with the word of God. If it is true prophecy, other Christians will recognize it as such, and your theology and life will confirm their recognition. Prophecy is not fortune telling. Prophecy is the Lord choosing to share His intention with you and bring His word directly to His people. If we are open to the Lord and desire to be used by Him we should not be afraid to speak the words or face the evaluation by the believers. Otherwise, we quench the Spirit.

Many people get a word from God but discount it as something that just happened to cross their minds. Whenever we are open to the Spirit, He will work in unexpected circumstances. Recently a man whom the Lord has been dealing with told me at our morning breakfast after daily communion that he wanted laying on of hands for the baptism of the Spirit at our next "Growing in the Spirit" meeting. We always end the breakfast by holding hands in a circle and giving sentence prayers. One lady there who had been divorced had said that she had been praying for three years that God would send her a husband. She wanted to be married and wanted her children to have a father. She said that she had tried to stay in touch with the Lord and be obedient to Him, but she couldn't understand why her prayers had not been answered. As we prayed our closing prayers, the man who wanted the full release of the Spirit in his life began to feel cold, and his knees begin to shake, and out of his mouth came the words, "A good farmer, after a good crop, allows the field to lie fallow before putting in another crop." He didn't know where these words came from, but after the evaluation of the other believers, this was taken as a prophecy of promise for the lady and as proof that the man had already experienced the baptism of the Spirit. The feeling of joy and relief that both of them experienced was also confirmation. Since this only happened last week, I cannot report to you that the lady has found that husband, but I'm willing to bet that she will.

Tongues! The most controversial and criticized of all the gifts. Because of misunderstanding, wrong teaching, fear, and ignorance, some people believe that tongues is the result of fanaticism, emotionalism, or the devil. People tend to criticize what they do not understand.

All the other gifts of the Spirit are for the edification of the Christian assembly, but tongues is the only one that is primarily for the edification of the individual. The purpose of tongues is to glorify God. It makes sense that God would give this gift if a person will take a few minutes to analyze why. After one has said, "How great Thou art," "Praise the Lord," "Alleluiah," and a few other stock phrases, what can one say in his own language? If praise is meant to be the main part of our prayer life, we obviously need some help, and this is what God has provided.

St. Paul says that it is the least of the gifts, but then says that he wishes that all would speak in tongues. I do not believe that tongues are denied to any Christian, but neither do I believe that all Christians must use this gift. The essence of conversion and the essence of the baptism of the Holy Spirit is surrender. There is something humbling about both of these experiences;

something brutal happens to our pride. The hardest part of ourselves to surrender is the tongue. St. James, in the third chapter of his letter, says: "So the tongue is a little member and boasts of great things. How great a forest is set ablaze by a small fire. . . . For every kind of beast and bird, of reptile and sea creature, can be tamed and has been tamed by humankind, but no human being can tame the tongue—a restless evil, full of deadly poison. With it we bless the Lord and Father, and with it we curse men who are made in the likeness of God" (vss. 5-9). Then, in the fourth chapter, he says, "Submit yourselves therefore to God. Resist the devil and he will flee from you. . . . Humble yourselves before the Lord and he will exalt you" (vss. 7-10).

Speaking in tongues is a precious gift from God. It is a different and intimate way of praying with direct, supernatural help once the person has surrendered himself to God. This, of all the gifts, has been the most abused. For some people, this has become a source of pride as they say, rather condescendingly, "I'll be so glad when you've received what I have," or "Everyone is supposed to speak in tongues, so you must not have received the Holy Spirit." Because their baptism in the Spirit has not issued in love, they tend to make other people who do not speak in tongues feel like second-class Christians. God's gifts are never useless, and they are never divisive. If their manifestation becomes divisive, you can be sure that someone is allowing the devil to work. Many ministers will tell you that their ministry deepened, spread, and became more effective once they allowed the Spirit to be released in their lives—with or without the manifestation of tongues. When it is authentic, lives begin to change for the better in a dramatic way. Groups who allow Jesus to be Lord and allow the Holy Spirit with all His gifts to have a free hand in them as individuals have found that attendance, giving, involvement, outreach, and worship have increased amazingly. All the gifts are designed to equip Christians with supernatural power to wage an effective battle against Satan, to spread the gospel, and to recruit others for the kingdom under the Lordship of Jesus Christ.

I urge you not to feel like an underachiever in the Christian faith, not to feel that you are some kind of second-class Christian if you do not speak in tongues. But be careful not to be too rigid to allow the Holy Spirit to work in your life—any way He chooses to.

The only times I have ever known the gifts of the Spirit to become divisive are when the doers and don'ters want things done their way. It is original sin rising up within the body. If the minister is against the whole business, condemns it, and turns his back on it, some of the members are left on their own. When this happens they often get way out in left field, feeling as though they are the "real" church while the ministers and the others are merely "playing church." The same sort of division can occur if the minister has a release of the Spirit in himself—including tongues—while the majority of the members are completely against this sort of thing and want no part of it. When this happens the people are divided, God's work is hampered, and the devil is delighted.

I am convinced that if both clergy and laity would only "hang loose in the Lord," Jesus' prediction that "the things that I do and even greater things than these will ye do" would come true to a degree that passes all human imagining.

Finally, the interpretation of tongues—the equivelent of prophecy. Tongues is a private devotional language for personal edification and praise of God with no interpretation needed. First Corinthians says: "For one who speaks in a tongue speaks not to men but to God; for no one understands him, but he utters mysteries in the Spirit." When tongues are spoken in public, there must be interpretation. Public speaking in tongues needs interpretation, for through this God may be speaking to unbelievers as well as to believers. Interpretation is not translation. It is meaning being brought to what has been said, for edification, exhortation, and/or comfort, as St. Paul tells us in I Corinthians 14:3-5.

There is no progress in the Christian life except by faith. Through the various gifts, the Holy Spirit is moving to show God's purpose and power among people. Tongues and interpretation of tongues are signs to believers and unbelievers when they are manifested according to scriptural instructions. They have the same benefit as prophecy, and they are for the edification and the building up of the Christian Fellowship.

When I was a kid it was fun, and just a little bit scary, to go out to some "Holy Roller" church and peep in the windows to watch the "goings-on" going on. It was

44

fascinating to watch them yell, dance around, and roll on the floor. Watching and hearing them left an indelible impression on me. From what I have learned, I am far from being the only person who has observed this kind of church meeting. Evidently, many share the misgivings I had about this kind of unrestrained religion. I am convinced that this is why so many people today are scared, or at least leery, of tongues and many of the other gifts of the Holy Spirit. I don't know what was happening at those Holy Roller churches— but I'm certainly not going to say that those people were not in contact with God, the Holy Spirit. It may have been pure emotionalism, or it may have been a mixture of emotionalism and the effects of the Holy Spirit, but it may also have been that they were so completely yielded to the Holy Spirit that they were in a trance-like state similar to some of the prophets of the Old Testament.

Thank God I have almost, through Jesus Christ, overcome my tendency to judge, label, and stereotype the religious practices of other people and denominations. I do know that many times they are reaching people that I could never reach with my ministry in my denomination.

I am positive that if your idea of the charismatic movement and the manifestation of the spiritual gifts is one of Holy Roller-like ecstasy, you are laboring under a delusion. But, if this is the case I can also understand why you might get uptight when you hear of the gifts, including tongues, being manifested in the Episcopal, Presbyterian, Methodist, Roman Catholic, and other "mainline" denominations. On the other hand, to see healings and miracles take place certainly is attention-getting. To hear people speak and act with supernatural knowledge and wisdom certainly should make a person think. And, to hear highly respected doctors, lawyers, business men and women, teachers, and educated, influential people—including nuns, priests, and ministers—prophesy, discern spirits, speak in tongues, and interpret tongues, prevents anyone, except those with completely closed minds, from discounting all this as ignorant, satanic emotionalism. Incidentally, to hear a group of people "sing in the Spirit" is to immediately supplant Guy Lombardo and his Royal Canadians as dispensers of the "sweetest music this side of Heaven."

I urge you not to knock something unless you've tried it. Don't be down on something just because you are not up on it. We are living in an age that urgently needs all the help we can get from God in order to combat the onslaught of evil that is being experienced in our society. With more and more people being "turned on" to the Lord, it is only natural that the devil would work harder and more dramatically to counteract this. This is why we are seeing such a growing interest in various cults and the occult. Such things as belief in reincarnation, Karma, metaphysics, ESP, astrology, sorcery, mind expansion attempts, and spiritualism are some of the ways that the devil is trying to snatch people away from God. Unfortunately, he is being successful with many, but at the same time there are more people turning to Jesus Christ than there have been for decades—perhaps, ever. The sooner Christians accept the fact that there is a battle going on for human souls, the sooner God's church will, indeed, start moving "like a mighty army." All over the world, and particulary in America, this is happening. God is being glorified in the commitment, faith, and lives of many of us who profess Jesus Christ as Lord and Savior, "as we are opening ourselves" to the power and work of the Holy Spirit.

PRAYER

There have been so many excellent books written on prayer that it seems presumptuous to attempt to discuss this subject in one chapter. However, since prayer is such an important fundamental of Christianity, it seems absolutely necessary to include some comments on prayer in a book such as this.

There seems to be more interest in and less understanding about prayer than anything else connected with Christianity. There are so many people whose prayer life is limited to moments of desperation, or "foxhole" praying. They are usually the same people who have not progressed in their spiritual growth beyond "God is great, God is good . . ." as a blessing and "Now I lay me down to sleep . . ." as a nighttime "sign off" to God. I believe this is so because prayer always expresses our relationships to God. The way we pray always corresponds to how we think of God. There are many ways of picturing God, and our prayers are shaped by our concept of Him. If we see God as a celestial "Super-cop," our prayers will differ from someone who thinks of Him as a kind, old grandfatherly type. Then too, just as our relationships with people change, our relationships to God are subject to change also. We are foolish to expect our prayer life to always be the same. If and when our understanding of

God and His purpose for our lives changes, our prayer life will change as well.

Our prayer life is also affected by the ordinary changing moods that all of us experience. Most of us pray completely different types of prayer when we are in different kinds of moods. Because of the problems that our human natures cause us in the area of prayer, the early church "fathers" compiled a list of five classic aspects of prayer. They are (1) Praise—this is the highest rung of the ladder. It is praise to God simply because He is God and worthy of our praise. (2) Thanksgiving—the offering of thanks to God for specific acts of mercy, or gifts, to us. (3) Intercession— asking God to do something for some other person, or persons, or asking Him to intercede in some situation or event. (4) Confession—recalling our acts of dis- obedience, defiance, or omissions, confessing them to God and asking His forgiveness. (5) Petition—asking for something for ourselves.

Have you ever noticed which aspect of prayer we deal with the least? Most of us neglect the most important one, praise. The other four are man-centered, while praise is entirely God-centered. This says some- thing about original sin. Thanksgiving is in response to something God has done for us or for someone we love. Intercession is for some person, and it is usually for someone we love or are concerned about. Confession concerns our sins and asks that we be forgiven. Petition is a "gimme" prayer we ask for ourselves.

I think it is significant that as the renewed interest in and emphasis on the Holy Spirit has spread, so the praise aspect of prayer has come to the fore. More and more people are discovering an often forgotten or never known Christian truth: we are supposed to praise God for everything—good or bad. When we do this, it means that we trust God. It means that we believe that God truly loves us, wills the best for us, and even though we may not see the reason or know what the final outcome will be, we know that a God who loves us is in charge. Human nature says that it is ridiculous to praise God for bad things that happen or the terrible situations that arise. It doesn't make a bit of sense—but it works.

So many people seem to feel that we must keep God informed on things. God doesn't need information, He only wants our trust. Many people spend most of their prayer time filling God in on the details and telling Him how they want their prayers answered; and then it is "over-and-out" and no time is spent waiting for God to speak. That isn't prayer—it is not even a two-way conversation.

Although this five-way prayer design has not been used by Christians as much in recent years, it still offers an excellent framework for prayer. Normally, not all five aspects will be used every time we pray, but it can serve as a good checklist for us in thinking about our prayer life. If we consistently omit one or more areas when we pray, our prayers are unbalanced the way many teenagers who almost live on hamburgers and french fries are eating unbalanced meals. Our spiritual life is harmed in the one case, and our physical life is harmed in the other.

If you are wondering how to tell when your prayer

life needs renewing or revising, there are some questions to ask yourself that may provide guidelines. The first is whether your relationship with God seems real to you. Next, is your prayer life affecting your relationship with other people? It has been said that prayer does not change God—it changes us. Last, are you experiencing the power that Jesus promised His followers through prayer? Even one "no" to this list can mean that you are missing something in the life of prayer.

There are many things about prayer that we do not know. However, as Mark Twain said, "It isn't the things in the Bible I don't understand that bother me, it's the things I do understand." Rather than getting bogged down on the unexplained things connected with prayer, let's look at some of the things Jesus answered for us on this subject. Here are some of the most common questions people ask about prayer, with a brief comment on what answers the Bible gives them.

"If God knows everything, then He already knows what we need or want, so why pray?" Even the most cursory reading of the Gospels will show that Jesus not only prayed often Himself, but He also instructed His followers to do likewise. The epistles also make numerous references to the importance of prayer—for example, I Thessalonians 5:17 states simply, "Pray constantly." This does not mean to stay constantly on our knees, but to stay in a constant relationship with God. If Jesus Christ, the Son of God, felt it necessary for much private prayer, and corporate prayer in the temple and synagogues, why on earth do some of us think we can get along with a minimum—or perhaps none, except in emergencies. I am convinced that all of life is an emergency, and the "chips are always down."

For reasons we cannot understand, God has chosen to allow man to share in the bringing in of His kingdom through the work of prayer. Just as He allowed man to have dominion over the earth and the animal and plant life, with the power to subdue it, He has also allowed man a vital part in bringing the spiritual life of man under God's rule. He will not do it by divine fiat. Jesus' words in Matthew 7:7-11 can be understood in both of these areas. "Ask, and it will be given you; seek, and you will find; knock, and it will be opened to you . . . how much more will your Father who is in heaven give good things to those who ask Him!" Christians often use this quotation in prayer groups and in teaching about the spiritual life. It can also apply to God's instructions to man to "have dominion" over the creation. Scientists, physicists, inventors, and every person who has ever had any part in creating something has learned the need to ask, seek, knock—not just once or twice, but over and over. The same principle that has been found to be true in those situations will also be found to be true in the spiritual journey.

Another common question about prayer is, How long should I pray about a thing? How can I tell if God has said no, or if I should keep praying? Jesus used the story of the importunate friend (Luke 11:5-10) in teaching the need to continue in prayer. According to this parable, a man was awakened at midnight by his friend who wanted to borrow three loaves of bread. The sleepy man told his friend to leave him alone—that he and his children were already in bed, and he didn't want to wake his whole household by getting up and giving him the bread. Apparently, the man at the door continued to knock and call his friend. The story says that although he wouldn't get up as an act of friendship, he finally did get up because of the man's persistence. I believe that Jesus used this story to teach us to persevere. I do not believe that it should be taken as a teaching on the nature of God, however, because verse thirteen of the same chapter states, "If you then, being evil, know how to give good gifts to your children, how much more will the heavenly Father give the Holy Spirit to those who ask Him!"

All of us have a tendency to avoid praying when we "aren't in the mood"—when we feel far away from God or when we feel we have prayed for a long time without hearing any answer. I believe that Matthew 9:12-13 can be used as directions to us in these times. It says, "But when he [Jesus] heard it, he said, 'Those who are well have no need of a physician, but those who are sick.' Go and learn what this means, 'I desire mercy, and not sacrifice.' For I came not to call the righteous, but sinners." Too often Christians are harder on themselves than Jesus is. If we recognize our state at these times, which is one of spiritual sickness, we can take seriously Jesus' statement that God desires mercy not sacrifice and can apply it to ourselves. Instead of feeling so guilty that we run away from God, which only makes us feel more guilty and miserable, we can quite simply present ourselves—with all the "bad feelings"—to God.

Let Him deal with it, and we can stop worrying about it. When we do this we feel a sense of peace that is our assurance that we really have turned the matter over to God. It is when we decide to handle it ourselves that we lose this peace.

Along with the above question goes the one, "What do I do when I just can't seem to hear God even though I am asking Him for direction?" There are times in everyone's life when God does indeed seem to be silent. Here, too, our Lord has gone before us and given us an example to follow. In the account of Jesus in the Garden of Gethsemane (Matthew 26:39-44), we see that three times Jesus prayed, asking God to "take this cup from me," while affirming His willingness to do the Father's will. Three times God was silent. Many of us can identify times when we have prayed similar prayers: "God, I really do (or don't) want to do this particular thing, but at the same time I want your will in the matter done. Please give me an answer one way or the other." What did Jesus do when each time God was silent? He made His own decision and then acted upon it. Verse forty-six tells of His saying to His disciples, "Rise, let us be going; see, my betrayer is at hand." Jesus' decision was probably based upon His knowledge of scripture (He was familiar with the predictions of a suffering servant as the Messiah), upon His wanting to do God's will, and upon the circumstances at hand—Judas and the soldiers were approaching. Our decisions can be based upon similar data. We can use our intelligence to discern what the Bible says, either specifically or in general, about the matter for which

54

we want a decision. We can use our knowledge of how God has acted in our lives in the past, as well as how we know Him to have acted in history in the lives of others. We can look at our present circumstances. Then, after we have prayed about it, we can make a decision and act upon it. I am convinced that *a Christian cannot make a wrong decision, if he is making it for the glory of God.* If it is the right decision, God will honor it. If it is the wrong decision, God will redeem it. Christians make wrong decisions all the time, but if the decisions are made with the idea of glorifying God or trying to do His will, God will right them every time. The key phrase is "to the glory of God." Let me give a little example that may help illustrate this. Let's say that you are a Christian businessman. You have two men working for you, and one of them must be fired. They are both equally competent, and both need the job. If the businessman reads the Bible looking for direction and prays fervently for an answer but cannot get any leading whatsoever, he should make a decision and carry it out. If it is the right one, God will honor it, and if it is the wrong one, He will redeem it in such a way that everyone will benefit all around.

In conclusion, I would like to mention briefly some hindrances to prayer. These are not necessarily in order of importance, nor is the list complete. I do not believe any discussion of prayer is complete without recognizing that some things do block our prayers, however. Failing to forgive can lead the list. In Matthew 6:14-15, Jesus warns that "if you forgive men their trespasses, your heavenly Father also will forgive you, but if you do not forgive . . . neither will your Father forgive your trespasses." An unforgiving spirit, harboring resentment or hurt, nursing wounded feelings, or acting as a self-appointed judge of the conduct of another person builds terrible walls between us and God, as well as between other people and us. It actually prevents our being able to receive God's forgiveness for our own sins. This, in turn, causes guilt feelings in us, sometimes specific, for things we know about, and sometimes worse—the vague, miserable feeling of guilt for something we can't even identify. This one problem—unresolved or unforgiven guilt—does inestimable damage mentally, physically, and spiritually. Unresolved guilt of our sins and resentment toward others can literally make us sick. All of us need to examine ourselves periodically to find those incidents where we have failed to forgive others and where we have failed to ask God's forgiveness for our trespasses. I believe it is vital to the spiritual life of Christians that they understand that when they pray the Lord's Prayer they are asking God to forgive them the way they forgive everyone else. It is arrogant to ask God to forgive us if we are not willing to forgive others.

Anxiety is another block to prayer. Here, too, Jesus gives definite instruction to "not be anxious" (Matthew 6:34). Like His admonition to forgive, though, this teaching is easier to hear than it is to obey. Anxiety is a form of not trusting God. There are different ways to combat it. One way is to recall instances where God has "come through" in your life—or in the life of someone you know. This is the theory of "if He has done it before, He can, and will, do it again.'' Reading some of the great affirmations of faith in the psalms or other parts of the Bible can also help, as can books telling of God's action in the lives of contemporary Christians. This is another reason why it is so vital that Christians witness. This encourages and strengthens the faith of others.

Disobedience and rebellion are two parts of the same thing—and another block to prayer. "Rebellion" sounds rather old fashioned. The Old Testament speaks often of it. I Samuel 15:23 states flatly: "Rebellion is as the sin of divination, and stubbornness is as iniquity and idolatry.'' Our rebellion leads to our disobedience. "Divination" is the divining of spirits, or witchcraft. Galatians 5:20 lists both idolatry (chasing after other gods) and witchcraft as "works of the flesh." In other words, both are forms of putting self in place of God; of wanting our own way, regardless; and ignoring God's directions for our life. It is easy to see how this can be a real block to our relationship with God and thus block our prayer life. It was rebellion and disobedience that prevented an entire generation of Israelites from entering the Promised Land—even after God had led them out of slavery in Egypt. It is often rebellion and disobedience that prevent us from entering the Promised Land of happy, abundant lives here on earth. If we block our relationship with God, it follows that we block our receiving the help and benefits He has promised to those who love and follow Jesus as Lord and Savior.

One more hindrance to effective prayer that I would

like to mention is "double mindedness." James 1:6-8 states that when we ask for something in prayer, we must ask in faith, without doubting, or we need not expect God to honor our prayers. The New English Bible puts it, "But he must ask in faith, without a doubt in his mind; for the doubter is like a heaving sea ruffled by the wind. A man of that kind must not expect the Lord to give him anything; he is double-minded, and never can keep a steady course." This passage is actually referring to a person who is asking God for wisdom, but I believe it applies to anything. We usually ask for wisdom because we need to make a decision as to a course of action or because we feel we need help to do some job that is before us. I believe there are several points here to be considered. The most obvious, of course, is to have faith in God's ability and desire to answer our prayer. But in addition, we are being told that we must be sure in our own mind just what it is we want. Do we really want God to impart His wisdom to us? What if this means we have to do His will in the matter, even though it clashes with what we think we want? We all know how frustrating it can be to deal with a person who can never make up his mind or who keeps changing his decision. Children who are the victims of parents who are habitually inconsistent in their discipline and care always show the adverse effects of this. If a business man shows this trait, his business invariably suffers. All of us know of examples of people who are "double-minded," and the havoc this can wreak in situations. No wonder we are warned against this in our prayer life!

Finally, I Peter 3:7 warns that, "you husbands must conduct your married life with understanding; pay honor to the woman's body, not only because it is weaker, but also because you share together in the grace of God which gives you life. Then your prayers will not be hindered" (NEB). There is tremendous prayer power in couples who are in accord with each other. Too few married couples realize that they do, indeed, share together in the grace of God, and it is this grace that gives them, and their marriage, life. There are probably many Christians today who wonder why their prayer lives seems so lifeless, but they have never considered looking at their marriage for an answer.

There are three things that I have mentioned in this chapter that hold the key to a successful prayer life:

1. Prayer always expresses our relationship to God. Our relationship to God should be likened unto the relationship of a small child's to a loving human father. A small child doesn't hesitate to ask anything of his father if he knows his father loves him. He knows that his father will say yes, no, or not now. The important thing is that their relationship is such that he feels completely free to ask. In the same way, our prayer life will be in accord with our relationship to God.

2. A Christian cannot make a wrong decision if he is making it for the glory of God or with the intention of doing God's will. God will honor it if it is right, and He will redeem it if it is wrong.

3. It is absolutely useless to pray if you do not expect God to answer. So many people pray prayers of petition or intercession, but do not really expect God to answer

them. This is only wishful thinking. This is not true prayer. We should ask, expecting—not just hoping for—a yes answer. We should also trust that if the answer is no it is because God wills only the best for us, and even if we don't understand the negative answer, we trust Him.

In our prayers that receive no as well as yes answers, in our prayers that seem to get only silence, we are to claim the promises of Jesus, and put our absolute trust in God, with our faith summed up in the title of a religious song, "I Don't Know What the Future Holds, But I Know Who Holds the Future."

THE BIBLE

In the present awakening within the churches of Christianity, like the great awakenings of the past, there is a fresh new discovery that the Bible is not just a book. People are discovering that it is the book through which God continues to speak to His people. Of course, millions have known this all along, but the exciting thing is new millions are beginning to realize this for themselves. Although it might sound corny to some people, the Bible is God's instruction manual for Christian living. In spite of the sophisticated world we live in, there is absolutely no situation that it cannot speak to, if it is read, studied, and prayed over. Obviously, if it is kept on a shelf unread, it is of little relevance to our lives! A fire extinguisher, properly used, can prevent a small fire from spreading and destroying an entire building. But if the occupant has never read the directions for using the extinguisher and is unable to apply its contents to the fire, the mere possession of the fire extinguisher is meaningless. What good are written instructions; what good is a "how to" manual if it is not read? What good is any kind of mechanism if one doesn't know how to operate it? The Bible is not something to be put on a shelf—not even in the highest place of honor. The Bible is not an object to be venerated. It is what the Bible teaches and who the Bible points to that makes it valuable. I have known people who feel somehow it is a sin to underline and otherwise mark up a Bible. That's exactly what we should do, at least to our personal Bible. As an age-old prayer puts it: "Blessed Lord, who has caused all holy Scripture to be written for our learning; Grant that we may hear them, read, mark, learn, and inwardly digest them, that by patience and comfort of thy holy Word, we may embrace, and ever hold fast, the blessed hope of everlasting life, which thou has given us in our Savior Jesus Christ."

People have always read the Bible for various reasons. The strength and dignity of the words comfort and inspire. In years past, the Bible was often the only book a family owned, so it was the sole source of reading material. People are rediscovering that the Bible is not just some history-like writings or some fairy tales of God dealing with some ancient people. They are finding that God is speaking to them personally in every situation in which they find themselves when they read His Word. Regular, disciplined Bible reading is for the Christian something like storing up nuts for winter is for squirrels. When they have done this and continue doing this they are able to reach into their storehouse and bring out some biblical truths that they can apply to particular problems in their daily life. Even skeptics find it difficult to deny the frequent coincidences that seem to occur when biblical truths are applied to modern-day situations and problems. The Bible has been called the greatest book on psychology ever written, but it is also the most practical book on how to live that was ever written.

The Bible is a record of God's action and man's reaction. The Old and New Testaments have often been called the old and new love stories of God for man. Because man does not change on his own and the Bible does record God's dealing with man, we can find ourselves throughout the entire book. The creation stories in Genesis point out our basic problem—wanting our will done regardless of the consequences. It is humbling to realize that on our own, we are Adam and Eve. We deliberately choose what looks good to us. "So when the woman saw that the tree was good for food, and that it was a delight to the eyes . . . and was to be desired to make one wise, she took of its fruit and ate." We decide against the best, which is obedience to God and living in His plan for us, and we opt for the "good"—only to discover, as Adam and Eve did, that we blew it. Then, still following the example of our illustrous ancestors, we immediately begin looking around to see who we can put the blame on. This sort of thing happens to all of us, over and over. It sometimes comes as a surprise to realize that all this is described in the third chapter of the first book of the Bible. In addition to describing man and his basic problem, the Bible also goes into vivid, lucid detail as to the consequences of man's declaration of independence from God. The Old Testament in particular is full of examples of what happens when man insists on living life on his own terms, ignoring God. The Bible never leaves us to clean up our own mess, however. It always goes on to point out the solution God has provided for us. In fact, the Bible teaches us the same basic truths in so many different, clear examples that, regardless of our background or mental ability, each of us should be able to grasp the truth for himself in ways that make sense to us.

More than likely, all of us have experienced the sensation of having been "cast out of Eden." This is the miserable feeling of rejection, of being alone, alienated from God, from our fellow man, and even from ourselves. Too often we fail to realize the root cause of this feeling, which is usually the result of our rebellious, self-centered behavior, our refusing to accept responsibility for our own actions, and our hiding from God. Incidentally, we can also find this recorded in Genesis 3:9-10: "But the Lord God called to the man, and said to him, 'Where are you?' And he said, 'I heard the sound of thee in the garden, and I was afraid, because I was naked; and I hid myself.'" We still don't care to stand in our naked state of rebellion before God. We still prefer to "hide" ourselves.

Once we learn to see ourselves in the Bible, we can go on to the next step, which is recognizing the specific directions for our lives. The Bible is so rich in truth about our human situation that, if we are really looking, we can find answers to problems even in Old Testament stories that appear totally unrelated to our present circumstances. One example of this is found in II Chronicles, chapter twenty. It is the account of Jehoshaphat, King of Judah and how God delivered his country from enemy armies. Chapter twenty opens with the news that three armies are coming against

64

Jehoshaphat in battle. This disquieting bit of information struck terror to the king's heart. Judah was a tiny country and totally unable to withstand such an assault. The first thing Jehoshaphat did (when he stopped shaking) was to call for a fast throughout the land and send for all the leaders to assemble and seek help from the Lord. Verse five describes where the assembly met, "in the house of the Lord." Jehoshaphat prayed, recounting God's past blessings to the people, reminding Him of His promises to them, confessing the helplessness of the assembled people in the face of the advancing armies, asking for help, and ending with the cry, "We do not know what to do, but our eyes are upon thee" (vs. 12). The next verse tells that the entire country stood waiting for directions from God—even the wives and little children. God spoke to the people through the prophet Jahaziel, who relayed the heartening promise, "Fear not, and be not dismayed . . . for the battle is not yours, but God's" (vs. 15). He then gave instructions as to exactly what the people were to do, which so encouraged them that they immediately began to praise the Lord. The next day they carried out their instructions, which were very simply to send out men before the army to sing to the Lord and praise Him. Verse twenty-two states that when the praisers began their songs, the Lord set an ambush against the advancing armies, and they were routed. What actually took place after this was that the enemy began fighting among themselves and destroyed each other without the small army of Judah even having to get into the battle. Many Christians today have discovered that the principles of this story can be applied to their problems with the same results. This "plan of action" has been tried by people today when faced with seemingly insurmountable odds, and found to be valid. First, look to God. Focus your attention on Him. Fasting (doing without food for a designated period) is an excellent way to do this. Somehow fasting always seems to draw our attention away from ourselves and onto God. Next, recall His past actions in your life. If you aren't conscious of anything specific, stop and think about your life. Many times we fail to recognize God's working in us. Now, admit your need. Ask Him to help you. Then, believe He will, and praise Him—even before you see the answer. Continue to praise Him and to trust that He is in complete charge of the matter.

Let me give you an example of this. I have deliberately chosen a simple, not overly serious one because too often we tend to think that it must be some tremenduous miracle if we are to give God the credit. There is a beautiful example of this in what happened to a friend of mine. To help tell about it, I will give the various characters fictitious names. Jane Wallace was the nextdoor neighbor to Frances Johnson. Their children got along like "cats and dogs." This is not too unusual except that both Jane and Frances were committed Christians. Frances, being a good mother, kept getting involved with the frequent arguments between the two sets of children. This, of course, only added fuel to the trouble. As the situation worsened, Jane asked a committed Christian friend of hers, Elizabeth, to go with her to call on Frances to see if things could not be smoothed out. Elizabeth loved her friend, so she prayed about it but received no confirmation that she should get involved. She searched her Bible hoping for some direction. Finally, she came to the fifteenth verse of the eighteenth chapter of the Gospel according to St. Matthew. "If your brother sins against you, go and tell him his fault, between you and him alone. If he listens to you, you have gained your brother." Elizabeth told Jane that this was saying to her that Jane should go and confront Frances by herself. Jane accepted this as a word from the Lord. She went to Frances, and the result was a complete healing of the relationship. I don't know whether or not this solved the problems between the children, but at least the two women were united in their desire for peace.

Now, I realize that anyone can use the Scriptures to prove any point. But when people seek the will of God in Scripture, God speaks to them and answers their questions, and if they obey Him, He heals their problems.

I have deliberately used examples from the Old Testament first—partly because Christians sometimes overlook this part of the Bible, preferring the more obvious guidance found in the life and teachings of Jesus. More and more people today are finding that the Old Testament stories have truth for their lives, and the wisdom and direction found in such books as the Psalms, Proverbs, and the books of the prophets never become outdated.

The Old Testament points to and predicts the coming of Jesus Christ. In addition to this important function, it can also be an invaluable aid to us in understanding our basic nature, and in realizing our need for a Savior. The New Testament records the fulfillment of the predictions and promises of the Old Testament. It introduces us to the Person of Jesus Christ, through the Gospel accounts of His life and ministry and through the later epistles to the young churches.

There are various ways of studying the Bible and many excellent study guides. As I said earlier, the Bible is an intensely practical book for Christians. In it we can find answers to any questions we can ask about ourselves. What makes it fresh and ever new is that when God speaks to us in the Bible, some passages that we have read perhaps dozens of times leap out at us the way words in fine print do when a magnifying glass is placed over them. Sometimes we can say, and really mean, "I don't ever remember reading that before." If that happens to you, pay attention, for God is speaking to you. It is, of course, possible to approach the Bible in such a scholarly way that we miss the value of its contents to our personal situation. This is unfortunate and unnecessary. It is true that in recent years there seems to have been an exciting new game that is popular among many theologians called "Demythologizing the Bible," or "We can't really be sure of the accuracy of the Bible." It is important to remember that the Bible is the Word of God—not necessarily the "words" of God. It is inconceivable to me however that Almighty God would go to all the trouble and pain of sending His only Son to earth, as fully God and fully man, and allow Him to grow up, teach, minister, die, and be raised from death in order to bring us back into a relationship with Himself and then allow the record of this to be "misquoted or distorted by the people He inspired to write it. It seems that many Bible scholars' real desire is to catch God in the wrong. They act upon the principle of "if I can't accept it, it must be wrong." Many times they don't seem to be trying to hear God speak through His Word. They seem to be trying to correct what they consider errors. I do not doubt for a minute that the Bible is totally trustworthy. I do not believe that God dictated the Bible, but I do believe God the Holy Spirit inspired the biblical writers to record the truth about the natures of God and man, and God's dealing with man, and I believe it stresses "man's need and God's action," to use the title of Ruel Howe's book. If we will read God's Word, asking Him to speak to us in it, His instructions will be as clear as the directions on the fire extinguisher that we spoke of earlier.

THE MINISTERING BODY

It is easy to understand that Jesus, the Holy Spirit and His gifts, prayer, Sacraments, and the Bible are part of the armor of God, but it is not so readily clear that the church itself—the fellowship of believers—is also part of the armor that a Christian needs in order to do the Lord's work. It is impossible to be a Christian by oneself—except in name only. We need the Christian fellowship as much as we need the more obvious helps that God has provided to aid us in being the people of God and doing the work of God. There is awesome power in the corporate body of people who are possessed by the Holy Spirit. Even the most committed Christians have occasional dry spells, and when these occur we need the faith and encouragement of other Christians. Jesus did not come to form a bunch of "me and God" individual units. He came to establish a community, a family. This atmosphere and under-standing is lacking in many parishes, and because it is, their effectiveness is greatly diminished. It is within the Christian body that we minister and are ministered to so that the members can reach out to the lost, the unchurched, and the floundering, whom Christ also died for, and wants for His kingdom.

In the early church, as best I understand it, the church had three functions: to worship God, to minister to the individual members, and to send out missionaries to recruit for the kingdom. I believe that these things are still the three functions of the church. The early church was not involved in social action; it was not an organized force dedicated to doing away with slavery and slums. It also was not a political force in the community. It had not pledged itself to raising the standard of living for people, bettering working conditions, nor to many of the things that some people today, in the name of the church, have often gotten bogged down in or obsessed by. Of course the church should be concerned about injustice, poverty, and discrimination. But, the church is in the business of changing the lives of people through allegiance to Jesus Christ, the love of God, and the power of the Holy Spirit. When people accept the Holy Spirit, when they have the nature of Christ and follow Jesus as their Lord, they are driven by love for their fellowman. One of the purposes of changing people from the inside out is to enable them to respond to the needs of the world around them.

The church is meant to change and equip people who in turn will change the world, through the life, teaching, and nature of Jesus Christ. The church—when it is truly the church—is the enabler of Christians to minister to the world's needs. The Christian is called to stand with one foot in the area of honoring and worshiping God and with the other foot in the area of serving God by serving His children. Now, after having said that, I must say that I am convinced that the world's real needs stem from spiritual problems more than material ones. In previous eras when the social gospel was in full sway, its proponents were convinced that if they could just clean up the slums and provide everyone with a job, the kingdom would come in. Unfortunately, they forgot what causes slums in the first place. Slums and poverty are the result of sin. The principles of "I want what I want when I want it," "I'm number one in my world," and "I want my way, regardless of whom it may hurt," are the essence of original sin, obsessive self-love, and self-centeredness. If the sinful, greedy people who are the cause of slums and poverty and the sinful people who are the victims are not both healed spiritually, there can never be permanent correction. This spiritual illness is "sickness unto death," and it affects people on all levels of society. At the risk of giving what sounds like a too simplified, pat answer, I must say that Jesus Christ is the only medicine that can heal this kind of sickness. Anything else is like putting bandaids on the ravages of cancer. It is human nature that is diseased. It is the world without God that is sick unto death. Until the causers and the victims have both had their lives and natures changed by committing themselves to Jesus Christ, Christians who have put on the armor of God must minister to them.

All of that is in the area of outreach and service, and this is necessary because it is in response to what Jesus has told us to do, but the church has a critical need to minister to its own members. It is intended to be a ministering body—not just a group of like-minded people who meet on a more or less regular basis for corporate worship. The description in Acts 2:44-47 of the early church gives a vivid picture of the ministering body: "And all who believed were together and had all things in common; and they sold their possessions and goods and distributed to all, as any had need. And day by day, attending the temple together and breaking bread in their homes, they partook of food with glad and generous hearts, praising God and having favor with all the people. And the Lord added to their number day by day those who were being saved." A common belief in the Lord Jesus drew the followers together into a living organism. They shared not only their lives, but their possessions with each other, they worshiped together, they had fellowship in their homes, and they praised the Lord. The Lord blessed their display of active love. This life-style was a witness to the community—"having favor with all the people"—and others were attracted into the church fellowship. I believe that the churches today (and throughout history) that have generally followed this pattern are the ones that have grown and will continue to grow and serve God and man. The early Christians ministered to each other first and then reached out to others. This is not a self-centered approach, but the common sense idea that spiritually and materially healthy people can more efficiently minister to the spiritually and materially poor. Also, it is natural to feed your own family first. This is as true in the Christian family as it is in our individual human family. After all, love is the tie that binds us to one another.

The church periodically needs to be reminded that it

is the Holy Spirit who enables people to serve God. Every Christian should be a missionary to those he comes in contact with in the daily business of living. It is in ministering to others that Christians learn to depend upon God for guidance and help. It is in listening to the Holy Spirit and stepping out in faith that people are able to discover their talents and gifts. As we exercise our talents and gifts they grow and develop. The ministering body provides the setting and climate that allow this kind of learning and growing to take place. Ephesians 4:1-16 gives an excellent blueprint for a ministering body: "I . . . beg you to lead a life worthy of the calling to which you have been called, with all lowliness and meekness, with patience, forbearing one another in love, eager to maintain the unity of the Spirit in the bond of peace. . . . And his gifts were that some should be apostles, some prophets, some evangelists, some pastors and teachers, to equip the saints for the work of ministry, for building up the body of Christ. . . . We are to grow up in every way into him who is the head, into Christ . . . when each part is working properly, makes bodily growth and upbuilds itself in love."

The Christian life is one of growth. Baptism is birth into the new life, but we must not stay spiritual babies. Growth in our spiritual life is similar in many ways to growth in physical life. Just as our bodies are constantly in a state of growing; recreating cells, taking in nourishment, throwing off waste, and maintaining the proper stability and health for each phase of life, so our spirits are always in a state of change. Unfortunately, we are usually more aware of our bodily needs than of our spiritual needs. Our spirits need to be fed through prayer, sacraments, Bible study, and sharing with other Christians. There needs to be discipline in our spiritual life fully as much as in our physical life. We need to recognize and treat spiritual illness so that healing can take place in the same way that physical illness must be recognized and treated in order to have healthy bodies. A spiritually healthy person is actively interested in serving God by serving people.

Many people who consider themselves to be good church members assume that the church exists for the purpose of having their spiritual needs met. I have heard some people say that they do not go to church because they don't get anything out of it. "Getting something out of it" is not the primary purpose of worship. Worship is something that is done out of duty to and in reverence for Almighty God. It is also done in gratitude for the unmerited love He has shown and continues to show toward us. I'm afraid that arrogance and ingratitude are two of the greatest blocks to spiritual health.

There is a story told of a woman who died and went to heaven. During her earthly life she had always been accustomed to the best. She had expected people to defer to her, even in her parish. She was neither a "Martha" nor a "Mary," for prayer groups and the like were not her cup of tea, and working around the church was beneath her. She preferred to do her church work up front in the limelight, and what charity she did, she did in the role of "Lady Bountiful" rather than out of real love. When she arrived in heaven an angel met her and said, "I have been sent to show you to your residence." As they walked through the section of houses that were much like the fine home she had lived in on earth, she kept wondering which one was hers. They soon moved into another section where the houses were not quite so elegant, but still highly acceptable. There, too, the angel did not stop but continued into a housing development of very modest houses. When he didn't stop there the lady began to get worried. Finally they reached a large area of tar-paper shacks, and the angel pointed to one of them and said, "This is yours." The lady indignantly responded with, "I can't live in this." And the angel replied, "I'm sorry, but this is all that we could build with the material that you sent up to us." I sometimes wonder what kind of eternal dwelling place they are constructing with the material I am sending up. Our heavenly home is built with the active love we show toward people in response to Jesus' commandment. There are many people like this lady who never understand that Jesus called the church into being in order that His ministry and mission to the world would continue.

When Christians are willing to commit themselves to Jesus Christ and submit themselves to the Holy Spirit and to each other, they discover that they are molded into a group that fits the description of the church that the letter to the Ephesians speaks of. When the church body is like a family, each member is important. Each member is respected as an individual, and as one who is expected to be a contributing part of the corporate group. In a healthy family each member recognizes and respects the worth and ability of the other members, while at the same time being aware of their failings and shortcomings and being willing to accept the other members regardless. The bonds of family love are stronger than the irritations and frustrations that erupt from time to time within the family. This is the way it is within a ministering body.

Just as our individual family develops its own particular life-style and is never exactly like any other family, so each parish must allow the Spirit to develop it into the kind of group that will best meet the needs of its members and best serve to further the Lord's work. No group should attempt to copy another group, although it usually works out that there are common characteristics among different groups.

There are two guidelines that the Spirit seems to be impressing upon every group of people that I've heard of who are learning what it is to be a ministering body. The first is that Jesus Christ must be the Lord of the church. This sounds almost too elementary because the general assumption is that this is the foundation for all Christian churches. This is true in theory but not in practice. It comes as a real shock to realize, as many of us throughout the world are discovering, that Jesus is not Lord of a church unless He is Lord of the individual people in the church. It is a slow, sometimes painful, process trying to establish Jesus Christ as Lord of our lives and of our churches. We have the grace and help of the Holy Spirit, but He will not force us to change. This change has to be an act of our own free will. This business of dying to self is a day by day thing. Having the discipline and love of a group of fellow-strugglers is a tremendous help. Christianity is a mixture of individual and corporate growth and life. God is our Heavenly Father, but each of us must also say and mean, "Jesus is my Savior and my Lord."

The only way a parish can fulfil its calling to be a ministering body is to remember that it is a two-fold thrust. It has been commissioned by Jesus Christ to minister to those outside the fellowship. This involves service to a hurting world. As it attempts to meet the needs of people in the world, it must be convinced that the foremost need is that people meet Jesus Christ. The church has been called and sent to preach the gospel, teach the Christian truths, and heal the spiritually, emotionally, and physically sick. It is to offer love, forgiveness, and acceptance as it witnesses to the life-changing power of Jesus Christ. Its ultimate purpose is to bring as many people under the lordship of Jesus Christ as it can. It is vital that people know that life is greater, more satisfying and joyful under His lordship than it is when He is unknown or ignored. But it is only people who are experiencing this new kind of life who can gain and keep the attention of those who are not. This leads to the second thrust which is in reality the first thrust. The church must minister to those already within the fellowship before they will minister to the outsiders. They can only minister effectively through the power of the Holy Spirit and under the Lordship of Jesus Christ.

I praise God that the part of the body of Christ that

calls St. Bartholomew's in Nashville its "home," is developing into a ministering body. Those of us in it have been helped in our Christian growth in a number of ways—many of which I'm sure are also used in other parishes. One of the things that has most helped me personally is the discipline of attending Holy Communion each weekday morning at 6:15. This is followed by a continental breakfast, a daily devotional reading, and ended with sentence prayers by anyone who is led to pray. At the beginning it was a chore. I cheered myself with the thought that it probably would not last but a couple of weeks. After all, no one—especially Episcopalians—would get to church that early and that often for very long. We have been at it for over nineteen months now with no signs of stopping. We average about eighteen people each morning and have had as many as thirty-two. The whole thing is over in less than an hour, and it is amazing what beginning the day with the sacrament of the Eucharist can do for the rest of the day. I have also learned the real joy and strength of meeting daily with a group of Christians for fellowship and prayer.

Another help to me has been a weekly evening prayer and praise group. This, like everything else at St. Bartholomew's, is open to anyone. We have people who attend all our meetings who have no intention of leaving their church to become Episcopalians. Their participation is a blessing to us. In our "Growing in the Spirit" group we sing, study the Bible, and pray together. We minister to each other and witness to the group of how the Lord has been working in our lives.

St. Bartholomew's has an adult Bible class every Sunday between the two worship services. Almost one third of our communicant strength attends this Bible class. Ninety percent of the class enrollment is there every Sunday. In addition to this, St. Bartholomew's has a men's prayer group, a women's prayer and Bible study group, a book study group (Christian writings), a tape ministry of teaching tapes for anyone to listen to, a good library of Christian books, a bookstore with an excellent selection of religious books, and there is almost continuous teaching throughout the year on such subjects as the Lord's Prayer, the Creed, the Christian family, the Holy Spirit, and the Bible. There are enough different opportunities offered so that a person serious about wanting to commit his life to Christ or wishing to grow in his commitment should be able to find help in his journey. We also have a chapter of the Brotherhood of St. Andrew which is dedicated to service and to recruiting members for Christ's kingdom.

The second guideline that the Holy Spirit seems to be impressing upon Christians is the need to be "subject one to another," or to "submit yourselves to one another." We are still learning what this means. We have learned that first of all we must listen to each other. It has been said that to love is to listen, and we are finding that this is true. We have also learned that it means we must open ourselves to each other. "Submit" in this case means being able to lay our thoughts and/or problems before each other in the way that a bid is submitted for a contract. It sometimes means that we must confess our sins (our faults and failures if the word "sin" throws you) to each other. Naturally this means that we must pray for each other and allow others to pray for us. There are times when "submitting" to prayers can be a humbling thing. One of the things that has been hardest to understand is that we must trust the Holy Spirit to be able to speak through a fellow Christian whom we may not especially like. We are beginning to learn that in order to have authority we must be under authority. I am the spiritual "father" of St. Bartholomew's, but it is no dictatorship. When we all submit to one another it is tied in with being under God's authority. By this we learn to exercise the authority He has given to man. As I said, we are learning. There is so much to learn—and we seem to be underachievers much of the time. It is odd that this new way of being the church is the way that the church was intended to operate from the beginning. Somewhere over the centuries it has gotten off the track, but, thank God, more and more Christians are learning what it really means to be the Church. Some things we have to learn over and over—things like praising God for all things, good or bad, and the need for confession and forgiveness within the body, and trusting God in the face of things we cannot understand. This process of growing is a continual reminder to each of us how much we need each other and how good it is of God to provide so many helps for us.

We are not there by any means. We've got a long way to go, but like the popular song by the Mills Brothers, "It Ain't No Big Thing, But It's Growing." We have begun, and we are progressing almost daily. We are also seeing the results. I am convinced that when the church as a whole begins to truly minister to the members within the fellowship and they begin to minister to people outside the fellowship, then "like a mighty army *will* move the church of God."

THE AWAKENING LAITY

I am convinced that the middle or late 1960s will go down in history as the time when the church, as a whole, began to hear and clearly understand what God the Holy Spirit has been saying since the beginning of Christianity: *"You—the laity—'be' the church; be what I called you to be; be my people, in an active, worshipping, witnessing, obedient, ministering way."*

This has been God's intention ever since He called Abraham to leave his country and people and go to a strange land. There God would develop out of Abraham and his descendants a people through whom all nations would be blessed. Since then there has always been a faithful remnant who understood this. In all of Judeo-Christian history there have always been little "pockets of people" spread out over the world who understood what God's call really meant, but it has never been quite like what is happening today. Church history tells of wonderful and mighty revivals, awakenings and movements which have kept the church alive, revitalized it, or moved it forward. But today God's call is coming through with a newness, a fresh-sounding clearness, that is exciting, life-changing, and inspiring. The Holy Spirit has been working on and in the laity in such a way that they no longer will settle for passive pewfilling.

In the past, it has generally been the clergy exhorting, cajoling, and challenging the laity to deeper commitment, more active Christianity, and greater giving of time, talent, and money. Today, in many instances, it is the laity that is prodding, pushing, and sometimes dragging the clergy toward the real work and worship of the church. There is a great difference between church work and the work of the church. Quite often in the past clergy and laity have subconsciously felt that the clergy were supposed to do the work of the church while the laity were kept busy doing church work. Much church work is necessary on the part of both laity and clergy in order to have a smooth, efficient organization, but the work of the church is something else again. This requires personal commitment to Jesus Christ as Lord and Savior, a sincere desire for everyone to come under the lordship of Jesus Christ, and a willingness to be obedient in carrying out the ministry and mission that Jesus Christ has passed on to His church. This involves a personal witness to the life-changing power of Jesus Christ, a desire to spread the gospel, and active recruitment for the kingdom.

From the middle 1950s to the middle 1960s many of the clergy and some of the laity gave the impression that only when the church was out on the streets and involved in social protest and social work was it being the church. There seems to be something in human nature that insists on everything being an either/or proposition. Many individual parishes are divided between the Marthas and the Marys; the pray-ers and the doers. Not only that, but often each group sat in judgment on the other. Worship, prayer, and Bible study that do not lead to active concern for one's fellow man are pious pretensions, but social upheaval and improvement that are not done in the name of Jesus or for God are examples of humanism. After a decade of the social gospel, many Christians came to the realization that there is more to Christianity than just the social gospel. And other Christians faced the fact that Christianity entails more than prayer and Bible study. Even though much good resulted from that decade of social activity, in and by itself it was inadequate and incomplete. Something vital was missing. True commitment to Jesus invariably leads to active concern for one's fellow man, but concern for one's fellow man does not always lead to the important necessity of commitment to Jesus.

Today some seminaries and theologians seem to be concentrating on trying to explain away the miracles and mysteries of Christianity. They are declaring that there are no religious absolutes, warning against a child-like belief in the efficacy of private prayer, and warning of the dangers of prayer groups. At a time when many are calling into question the words and events of the Bible and emphasizing—to the point of deifying—man, the laity has discovered that miracles are happening daily, the Bible is as up-to-date as the morning newspaper, prayers are being answered, and that God in Jesus Christ can be known personally. A radical—but wonderful—change in the lives of people is always what happens when Jesus is held up, called upon, and worshiped and obeyed as Lord and Savior.

It was to shepherds rather than religious leaders that the angels announced the birth of Jesus. So many times intellect gets in the way of understanding and accepting the deep truths of Christianity and the wonderful way that God works. Jesus said, "Unless you turn and become like children, you will never enter the kingdom of heaven" (Matthew 18:3). He also said, "Whoever does not receive the kingdom of God like a child shall not enter it" (Mark 10:15). It takes child-like acceptance of salvation and belief in the Word of God to enjoy the full benefits of all that God has to offer. This is not to say that one should not have doubts and questions. Doubts should not be denied, and questions should not go unasked. I do not believe that there is anything in the Christian faith that will not stand up to doubts, questions, and investigation. There are many things connected with Christianity that may not make sense because of our limited knowledge with the ways of God. But, unless our minds are closed and we have already decided what God can or cannot do, will or will not do, it is possible for God to perform His miracles, speak to us through His Word, answer our prayers, and come into a personal relationship with us.

At the other extreme from the intellectuals who have such difficulty with the basics of Christianity are the people who insist that they have blind faith. This is often a cop-out because they are afraid that if they investigate Bible claims and find that they are not exactly what they have believed from their childhood, they will have nothing that they can believe in. They are afraid that if every word in the Bible was not "dictated" by God and cannot be accepted in what they consider a literal interpretation, then their faith will be shattered. I don't believe that this is real faith at all. The Bible is the Word of God, not necessarily the words of God, and if it is read, studied, and prayed over, it will speak to any problem or situation that arises. Praise God! More and more of the laity are discovering this to be true. In increasing numbers lay people are reading God's word, listening to Him speak to them through it, and are finding that it contains what they need when they need it. Many clergymen are discovering this also, and this is tremendous because, for good or evil, parishes tend to follow the leading of their pastor.

I have always seen the role of minister as celebrant of the sacraments and as coach and cheerleader to the people in the struggle against the forces of evil and in the spread of the kingdom. It is a matter of teaching and exhorting: "Yea, God!" and "Go sic 'em, laity!" Much of the church is finally realizing that she can fulfill her mission and ministry only as lay people accept the commission that the Lord has placed on His body.

It is not enough to live good moral lives. It is not enough to live by the Golden Rule. Jesus' call is a call to action. It is a call to love our fellow man—not only our fellow Christian but all others, even our enemies. It is also a call to war against the forces in opposition to God and His people. At the same time that we are called to be ambassadors for Christ, we are also called to be active soldiers in God's army. Ambassadors must know the person or group they represent. Soldiers must know whose they are and what the cause is that they are

87

fighting for. They also must be equipped for battle. Unarmed and unequipped, they are ineffective. When a person joins Christ's army, he takes the name of "Christian" and is supposed to put on the armor of God. Many have taken the Lord's name in vain and have failed to put on the armor of God. But the exciting thing that is happening today is that thousands of Christians are beginning to take seriously the vows that they made to God at their baptism and/or confirmation. They are claiming the gifts of the Holy Spirit, using His power, and enjoying the benefits He has provided. Both clergy and laity are allowing God the Holy Spirit a free hand to do His work in and through them. Jesus has become, to them, the Living Lord, and He is fulfilling in their lives the promises He has made.

Never on such a wide scale have people admitted, proclaimed, and witnessed to their commitment to Jesus Christ. Isn't it an odd development that it is "news" that Christians are beginning to acknowledge and act upon their professed commitment to Jesus Christ? In the past, many teenagers and adults have been hesitant to talk about their religion out of fear of their peer group's disapproval. Their religion was something they "did" on Sundays, but during the week it was pretty well put away. Oh perhaps it influenced their actions during the week, but it was something one just did not talk about because they did not want to offend others or risk their disapproval. All of a sudden, religion is respectable. Jesus can be talked about, witnessed to, called upon, without fear of being considered a religious nut, a goody-goody, or a square.

Some of the greatest Christians are athletes, entertainers, business and civic leaders, and politicians. They are not "closet Christians" who hide behind the claim that religion is a private, personal affair. Real Christianity must always be personal, but it cannot be private. Many people have turned to Christ and away from drugs and alcohol because they have found that He is the answer, the way to real living—the abundant life. They have found that He is the real mindbender, mind-expander, the real way out of the wilderness that many of them have been lost in for so long.

With all the spiritual renewal that is taking place, the devil is working harder and harder to lure people away from God. As long as people are nominal Christians—playing church with lukewarm commitment to Jesus Christ—there is no great need for increased activity on the part of evil. The devil can win by default. Although the ultimate battle was won on Calvary, many lives can be lost in the mopping-up campaign that has been going on since then. On the other hand, if people are beginning to be the church in more than name only, then the battlelines are drawn, and it is to be a fight to the finish. The devil is a powerful foe. He can counterfeit any of the gifts of the Holy Spirit. He can and will appeal to physical desires in order to get people under his power. He will use human intellect and pride as his active weapons. His greatest advantage is when he can get us to believe that he doesn't exist. His most potent tactic is to appeal to our physical desires, weaknesses, and self-centeredness.

Have you ever heard the expression: "Something is

as ugly as sin?" Don't you believe it! If that were true it would be no problem. Sin is as attractive and alluring as anything can possibly be. If it were not, it would hold no temptation and would be completely ineffective. The results of sin are ugly, but the appeal of sin is most attractive. The devil plays on our pride, our intellect, our emotions and desires, in order to lure us away from loyalty and obedience to Jesus Christ.

God has called His army, equipped it for its mission, and given His orders. He has issued a battle plan through His Word and given the power to carry it out. If we will put on the armor He has provided, the only other thing that is needed is our loyalty and obedience. He is counting on us to carry out the mission and ministry begun by Jesus. There is a story told of how after Jesus lived, died, and was resurrected, He returned to heaven. The angels asked Him how things had gone. He replied, "Not so good. I left the whole things in the hands of eleven people." The angels then asked, "What if they fail?" and Jesus answered, "I have no other plan." He has left the task in the hands of those who profess to belong to Him. If we don't do it, it won't get done.

The thing that excites me is the fact that so many of those who do profess to belong to Him are accepting the task He has given us to do. They are meeting Him personally, seeing His promises fulfilled in their lives, and are claiming the power that He promised to send. They are experiencing His presence with them as they begin to do all the things He said His followers would be able to do. In the past, so much of the church was dealing with secondhand information: the Bible says so-and-so, the church says such-and-such, and some people say that certain things have happened to them and in their lives. Today, thousands know these things from firsthand experience, the way the original disciples knew them.

This sometimes bothers some clergymen. Some are threatened by "turned-on" laypeople. If they themselves are dealing with second-hand information, they don't quite know what to do with people who know Jesus in a personal relationship. Several years ago I heard a bishop say that the church doesn't know what to do with a person who really gets turned on. Ushering, lay-reading, and the like just won't satisfy them. Thank God there are movements developing throughout the whole Christian church that are not only being the instruments through which the laity is being turned on, but are also helping them to grow, be nourished, and do the work of Christ's church. Renewal is sweeping throughout nearly all the various Christian denominations. Individuals and parishes that have seemed almost completely dead, are experiencing resurrection. Although these movements are primarily lay movements, many clergymen are involved in them as well. Faith Alive, Faith at Work, Cursillo, the Charismatic Fellowship, Lay Witness Weekends, Lay Renewal Weekends, Campus Crusade, Young Life, Youth for Christ, and Christian Athletes are but a few of them. The Full Gospel Businessmen's Association, The Brotherhood of St. Andrew, and the Fellowship of Witness are three other organizations or groups through which the Holy Spirit is causing renewal to take place. These thrusts are changing the lives of people, completely rejuvenating dead or lukewarm churches and making Christianity real and powerful in the world today. It is thrilling to see more and more churches beginning or increasing the number of prayer groups, forming "praise and witness" groups, and incorporating healing services as a regular and official part of the church's life and work. One-to-one witness and counseling are taking place between church members. Counseling and ministering is no longer the exclusive function of the ordained clergyman. The church is being the church because it is discovering that it cannot be the church unless the laity understand and accept the fact that every Christian is called into the ministry. The church's work needs the different talents and gifts of its members, and the different members have different functions. The ordained clergy have been set apart and equipped for special functions, but they cannot do—and are not supposed to do—all the ministry that the church has been called to do.

Lent is a church season that is designed for the purpose of looking at one's life, one's self, one's goals, and what one really believes in. It is forty days of increased reading of God's Word, concentrated listening for God to speak to us through it, through prayer, and through other people. As commitment deepens in people, the Lenten practices no longer end with the official forty days, but become the normal year-long way of life. This life becomes exciting, fulfilling, and wonderful. When people use the Lenten period for recharging their spiritual batteries, there is no letdown after Easter. The victory that Easter proclaims and the gift that Pentecost celebrates make the Christian life the exciting thing that the disciples and the other early Christians found so exhilarating.

If your church is not experiencing any of the renewal that is going on, if you are not seeing lives being dramatically and drastically changed, and if this excitement and joy is not a part of your life, something is wrong. Do you feel that your church is actively being the church as described in the Book of Acts? Are you personally and your church corporately experiencing the love of God in an obvious way? Are you and many of the others in your church claiming and using the power that Jesus promised to His people? If not, there is a reason. Something is blocking it, and it should be removed. No matter where you are in your spiritual life, there is always a next step, a higher plateau, a fuller revelation of God and His plan for His people. So many people settle for the fringe benefits of Christianity without experiencing it in its fullness.

Fringe benefits are welcomed, needed, and beneficial, but they remain fringe benefits. There is no point in trying to live the Christian life unless we have accepted Jesus as our Savior and are allowing Him to be our Lord, for that is what the Christian life means. There is no use looking to the church for advice unless we find out what the source of our problems is. If you would like to be an active Christian you must be prepared for a radical alteration in your life as you are led by and are obedient to the Holy Spirit. There is no participation in the life of the church unless we are bound to one another in love, and we will not know and experience the saving, healing power of Jesus unless we respond to His call, accept His forgiveness, and claim His power to be His instruments and witnesses in the world. Anything less results in lukewarm commitment that will dissipate when the going gets rough. It is only the people who surrender control of their lives to Jesus Christ who experience the new kind of life He offers. They are the ones who live on "tiptoe expectancy" greeting each day with the thought: "I wonder what God has for me to do and experience today." When we truly believe that God loves us, we know whatever situation arises and whatever challenge God places before us, we will be blessed by it, and He will be glorified if our response is one of eager obedience.

If this kind of faith and trust is fundamentalism, then so be it. This is the kind of fundamental faith that Jesus of Nazareth had and practiced. We as His followers are not expected to imitate the style of life of a first-century Jew, but we are to imitate His faith and obedience. God has chosen us, called us to be His people. If you have responded to His call, remember who you are, whose you are, and who you represent. I urge you to go forth in His name and with His power to be His witness and instrument in the world.